Off-Season at the Edge of the World

Other books by Debora Greger

And

Movable Islands

The 1002nd Night

Off-Season at the

Edge of the World

Poems by Debora Greger

University of Illinois Press   Urbana and Chicago

for *William Logan*

Publication of this
work was supported
in part by a grant
from the National
Endowment for
the Arts.

Designed by Richard Hendel

© 1994 by Debora Greger

Manufactured in the United States of America

P 5 4 3 2 1

This book is printed on acid-free paper.

Library of Congress

Cataloging-in-Publication Data

Greger, Debora, 1949–

    Off-season at the edge of the world : poems /

by Debora Greger.

      p. cm.

      ISBN 0-252-06380-5 (pbk.)

      I. Title.

      PS3557.R42O38 1994

      811'.54–dc20   93-30480

                                CIP

Acknowledgments

....

American Voice: "Miranda's Drowned Book"
Chronicle of Higher Education: "A Woman on the Dump"
Columbia: "The Dictionary of Silence"
Georgia Review: "A Field of Rape," "The Flowering Crab"
Gettysburg Review: "The Later Archaic Wing," "Vermeer"
Kenyon Review: "The Sadness of the Subtropics,"
   "Wind Wrapped in Snow"
The Nation: "Early Rome," "Like a Woman,"
   "Long Island Night," "Notre Dame des Tourists"
New Republic: "The Frog in the Swimming Pool"
New York Times: "Persephone in the West"
New Yorker: "The Afternoon of Rome,"
   "Air-Conditioned Air," "The Hustler de Paris,"
   "Invitation to the Past,"
   "Off-Season at the Edge of the World"
North American Review: "Ovid on the Outer Cape"
Paris Review: "Briar Rose"
Partisan Review: "Rilke in the Middle Ages"
Pequod: "The Garden,"
   "Les Très Riches Heures de Florida," "Three Graces"
Poetry: "Blue Mirrors," "The Boy Juliet,"
   "Cleopatra in the Afterworld,"
   "Under Cancer," part 1
Sewanee Review: "Tapestry," "Under Cancer," part 2
Western Humanities Review: "The Right Whale in Iowa"
Yale Review: "La Petite Danseuse de Quatorze Ans"

Special thanks go to the National Endowment for the
Arts and to the American Academy and Institute of
Arts and Letters.

Contents

"Love is the only thing that interests me," he said.

"The trouble," his uncle said to him, "is that without

river navigation there is no love."

—Gabriel García Márquez

Envoi

....

I open my stammering and unready lips
—Cosmas the Alexandrian

From here on it's hard to say whether you should
use oars or your mainsail
—Ovid

Here lies the Dutch galiot *Ver Meer*.
The *Maria Crowther* out of London and Gravesend,

J. Keats, Esq., aboard. A fleet of gulls,
scavengers all, preen in a parking lot's puddles.

Little wreck-chart, you're on your own now.
I'll think of you in a room the color of salt,

where one thin book's wedged under a table leg
to render an island immovable.

Where two, nearly spineless, lean against each other
and—and gather dust on a shelf.

The thousand and third night you're gone,
I'll think of you propping the window open,

your paper warped, sail bound nowhere in the salt air,
the young woman who wintered there

at Land's End gone. I remember the bay
blank with fog, blindingly blank.

Every day the road is longer,
past the six-foot lobster on the restaurant roof,

past the ghost warrior of the Samurai Motor Inn.
Go, little book. Find her. Tell her such happiness

as hers one day fails to exact its daily tears,
and what will she have to lose then?

Send back word.

Blue Mirrors

....

> blue mirrors, in which hidden laws reflectingly behold
> themselves, distances large like the future and like it
> unfathomable
> —Rilke

WITHIN

Blue is the sound that laps, that slaps the piers
until they're as blue as the sky

they loft a roof against, a blue so deep, so clear
only the ribs of ice-crystal cirrus would float

over the forest of stone where air is equal parts
cold, candle wax, incense, and mold: blue the hour

when into the chapel straggle the boy sopranos,
blue the last tease drowned by the organ's swell.

Who will be transported this evensong?
The wooden angels are dusty.

No call for a saint to walk away from death
over stained-glass waves when he can row

to the galleon outlined in lead,
hard by a milky iceberg anchored in wait

at the blue edge of the Old World.
In her window across the nave

a woman in red with a child on her hip
is turned away, what's left of her face

lost to all but Herod's soldier nearby.
Swarmed by children, one on his back,

one riding his armored foot,
he has become almost hers, home from a
    forgotten war,

though his gray eyes search not her but us, our
    firstborn.
Out from the trees in blue-green leaf

his comrade has stepped, raising a blue-white blade
to get on with the slaughter of the youngest boys,

the only red that's spilled
the shafts of light stained by the dress

the glazier gave her, light flashed with rubies
too rich for her rank spilling to the floor.

WITHOUT

Blue is the hour when into the orchard
of shadows drift the first deer,

blue the fruit they glean
in the long blue grass that blade by blade

bends under the weight of dew.
However you make yourself other than threat,

still, without lifting her head
from the shadows she grazes on,

the doe has stiffened into stone.
You will come no closer this blue hour.

With the slyness of the shy,
she has eased her body between you

on the old beach road and the fawn,
edging it along its shadow into the forest

of shadows until they are lost.
All you hear is down the cliff

where wave upon oncoming wave
batters and then licks clean

the black, the blue shore that crumbles
under such solicitude.

Deep as midnight are the halves,
mismatched, of mussel shells washed up,

one left cradling for the night
a spoonful of salt in its mother-of-pearl,

one overturned in the blue sand,
small craft aground, awaiting the turn

of the tide to rock it adrift.

Miranda's Drowned Book

Sit still, and hear the last of our sea-sorrow.
—The Tempest

The only potion I saw him brew was tea
of his own blend, a mash of leaves and bark.
Good for whatever ailed you was his claim,
as if he could see the leaps and falls
he'd named "the heart." Who knows?
                              For argument,
just say he had no need, had made me up:
one in his likeness, who wouldn't touch the stuff.
Who tried to see a window where he outlined
in air its air of distance, ladylike,
a pane designed to cut you off from the world
of the dunghill and the worm.

Who fashioned a cloak of leaves that aped his cape,
mine only as magic as waterproof, a screen
against the downpour day after day of sun,
unlike the one he wrapped in and became
no longer Father but some other, a stranger—
the island's only one—the local god,
or was it merely King of Somewhere Else?

Or mother country, I his colony?
He held forth promise of some other isle,
no drier but more "cultivated," not
just with crops but with quotation marks.
How he held forth, dutiful silence mine to guard.
I borrowed foreign names from the remains
of a map that washed ashore, my own worn out

through under-use. So, Carolina North,
or South? Virginia West?
                          As long as I
remembered not to answer to "Miranda!",
the call of parent bird to fledgling ingrate,
then I was not the heir apparent but
your normal castaway, a little bored
with ins and outs of tidepools' smelly courts.

Perhaps not world enough, but I had time
to watch a hermit crab align himself
and back into a vacant whelk and haul
the home he wore from rocky A to B.
All that watching—watching for what? A sail
blown off its course by my uncalled-for sighs?

A gorgeous morning, same as yesterday,
I in the same old shirt he'd handed down,
divining rightly that if it failed to fit,
a scabbard's belt would cinch it as a dress.
To the crab's new quarters a small limpet clung.
What did I want to be? What did I know
but him, the man who'd loved his subjects less
than his library, who'd lost his kingdom, who
couldn't put down a book he'd yet to finish?

How close the air remote upon that isle,
the like of which I have not breathed again.
How it held water, building up a wall
by keeping molecules apart. How close
those castles, not to be counted on except

to rumble, then to wilt late afternoons,
all squandered weakness.
                        Whatever I had sensed
about my difference I caught from him
or from the books he carried in his head.
Such dreams he made on me.
I am a leaf torn loose from his drowned book.
All men are islands, though they swear otherwise.
All islands are alike in their unhappiness.

Vermeer

....

Every seaworthy vessel a woman
whose mate, eloquent of how she handled
under the worst of weathers, hailed his goddess
of wet fire, handmaid and dockside whore.

Over the courtyard's dry dock, linens snapped.
Brisk was the wind that claimed divine right
to salvage whatever tore loose,
brisk at the docks the trade

in foreign plumage, and the milliner,
arms full of wings, who tripped in a puddle
that brimmed with sky. Past the known world,
past the map that decorated a room

with scalloped waters where ships the size
of fingernail parings were never snagged
by the dragon-sharp islands,
a keel of leaf scraped across a pane.

A branch scratched endearments on the air
it then brushed clean as sand.
Had the woman rereading a letter
looked to the window casting her light,

she could have seen almost to land's end,
the salt sea broken into semaphore
flashing its glassy code for tears
back to shore, seen almost to the cage on deck,

the pigeons gray as the mind,
some to bear messages home the first days out,
the rest to fatten in the hold.

Off-Season at the Edge of the World

We have crawled on our fins
from the sea into the sandy sheets
of the Holiday Inn.
How late we are to rise, how civilized,

who put on the furs of animals
against the seasonable chill.
Who walk on two legs down Commercial Street
past the petrified saltwater taffy,

the shops gaily boarded up.
By then it is midafternoon
at the end of the world, near dark,
time for a drink. The nights are long,

these the ones the ancients measured
fourteen fingers deep by water clock.
The room's a postcard, the view a stamp.
The ancients were right,

the earth's just driftwood, a slab of wood
adrift in a bowl of dishwater
under an overturned sky.
You empty your pockets:

from a two-fisted hourglass,
a little dune spills on the bed,
the racket immense,
grain against grain, wave after wave.

Parts rubbing each other wrong,
resistance wearing resistance down,
how civil we are to each other,
who have laid bare the law of friction,

skin sliding against skin
slick with the rigors of inventing pleasure.
I love you as I love salt, the ancients said.
Everywhere I lick you, you taste of it.

Three Graces

....

after Canova

In the dim tent they are dimmer still,
three elephants chained by the leg
one to the next, one to the ground.

Fogbound oceans, they ebb and surge
in a leathery tide. Lost in a rhythm
not even feeding stops, they rock again

the black hold of a freighter
tossed on open seas, the dark portholes
of their unblinking eyes unfathomable.

The tattered maps of their ears
flick away the local flies.
Nothing to them our incurious stares,

having no use for us who neither
feed them nor let them go.
There is no grace as dark as theirs.

The Right Whale in Iowa

The shag rug of a Great Plains buffalo,
   a flightless bird
gone to stone: over its fellow keepsakes,

    into the archives of air,
the whale hauled a harvest of dust.
   In the ripples of glass

sealed over songbird skins, I wavered.
   What could be said for love?
From the Full-Serv to the Self-Serv Island

    at the Gulf station next door,
landlocked waves shivered in a row of corn.
   The great flukes lifted.

A Milky Way scarred the underside more vast
   than the Midwestern night.
Dark cargoes would give themselves up

    to these shallows
that waited to take home the sailor,
   home to the sea

of fossilized coral upon whose shoals
   just down the road
the motels of Coralville lay sprawled.

    Here would lie a ring
scratched by a scrivener with florid hand,
   In thy breast my heart does rest

flung back to shore, here rest two coins
    face to face, joined
by the salt that turned them faceless

    as they turned to each other.

Long Island Night

A last swimmer fished himself out,
a final splash carried over waterlogged air.
    Left to its own devices,

your neighbor's pool burbled and glowed;
    an insect not quite cricket
rubbed its legs together, revving up to send

    the code all throbs and drones
that seeks a mate to shut it up. The tree whose name
    I, your westerner, hadn't caught

held forth upon the question, multiple choice,
    of a single bird that rattled off
a string of calls, not one its own. Mocking,

    you called it; I knew that.
Erie the inland sea whose shore we'd hugged
    most of a day on our way here,

you driven to ask, *Where wouldn't we be happy?*
    Into the swells of roses
the boat in the driveway leaned and groaned.

    Rigging slapped the mast
until it sang out, warning of thorns.
    Cold Spring Harbor

and Garden City slept, and you, my easterner,
    on your far coast of bed. Deep
in the light-spill that surrounded your *Good night,*

stars I'd pieced together
on another shore hid how they hurtled in place.
    What, between coasts,

was a little distance? What, between oceans,
    were a few tears? Deeper
into dream your boat drifted, past fields

    plowed into parking lots
where suburbs burned what neon they had,
    up a ramp to the L.I.E.

The Interpretation of Dream

....

What thou seest when thou doth wake,
Do it for thy true love take
—A Midsummer Night's Dream

THE INDIFFERENT MATERIAL OF DREAM

And in the dream a man I didn't know
was where my husband should have been in bed
beside me—was my husband except his face
was wrong, was longer and was velvet-furred.

One large brown eye stared off into the dark,
the other one regarded me as threat
or edible, I couldn't tell you which
but felt a great affection for him then

as wife might feel toward husband shaking her
from nightmare back to life, consoling her,
hushing her cries, "Shut up, it's just a dream."
Perhaps the purest pleasure is relief.

THE DISTINGUISHING CHARACTERISTICS
OF DREAM

But let me try those blots of ink again—
someone who read the clouds as snowcapped peaks
where there were only plains should see a face
with ease where there is none—the pointed ears,

the outsize toothsome grin or snarl emerge
from shadow as they did that night midsummer,
a bear in every bush, each stump a face.
A leafy hand would brush against my eyes,

a green-black heart with ragged edges lay
its less-than-perfect shape upon my sleeve.
Some humans slept a wild night off like logs
fallen across a trail, lying in wait,

unmoved, to trip a shadow like myself.

MEMORY IN DREAM

Or you and your wall of masks have it reversed.
Behind the hung-up faces, hollow-eyed,
that stare me down, laid out upon your couch
in deathly silence costing me the earth—

I've lost the thread for all my worrying
my sweater sleeve—behind the tiger's head
from Mexico, whose eyes are mismatched blue
and green, the marbles we called cat's eye, and

whose tongue hangs out, cut from red inner tube—
behind the raven's beak that's opened wide
to show the wolf it hides in its wooden throat,
there's nothing but a patch of wall that will

not fade or dirty, clean as countertops
the like of which a housewife's urged to dream.
Dream isn't wish. It's wish fulfilled that's dream.

WHY THE DREAM IS FORGOTTEN AFTER WAKING

Nor I the cleverest of your dreamers, nor
the most transparent? Don't answer that. You won't.
Who was the man who trotted in front of me,
holding a torch that failed to light his face,

his neck stretched forward in an attitude
of browsing as a grass-eating creature would?
What of the book that fell open in my lap,
a monograph my husband had dashed off

on the subject of my favorite flowers, weeds
you braid into a wreath only the most
besotted lover would agree to wear?
Dried and pressed, gone airmail-paper thin,

a specimen had been identified
in what might be your hand, illegible.
The binding matched your black appointment book.

THE RELATION OF DREAM TO WAKING LIFE

Yet in that dream before I woke, before
I saw the man whose head lay in my lap—
the beast whose furry ears I scratched behind—
for what he was, a man like any other,

that hairy nothing loose from someone's pen,
who rolled his big brown eyes in ecstasy's
fine frenzy, gave whatever I felt for him
no name. If it were love, I loved him then.

What would you call it? The locals have their word
and it is rude. For you, something more clinical.
Yet think of Garbo after she'd just seen
the movie *Beauty and the Beast*, the beast

by Beauty's love turned into Jean Marais,
a prince, a star all Gallic golden locks—
yet think of what the stories claim she said,
the five words quoted, "Give me back my beast."

Lives of the Saints

NOTRE DAME DES TOURISTS

And then one afternoon in Paris
you stumble on a church you can't find
in your guidebook, the more welcome

this late hour for that,
its air already incensed for centuries
by all that you'll all too soon let go—

its proper name, the name of any
but the pagan god Nike,
worshipped these latter days

down to his shoes. Off your worn feet
you immodestly ease his brand, toasting it
with a swig of mineral water you sneak.

Her statue stands on an altar, unmoved,
bare feet in guttering vigil lights,
the blue patroness of the halt, the lame phrases

led by the guardian angel Berlitz
back to earthly travail from the limbo of French I.
Blessed be the evensong unsung,

the confessionals empty this *cinq à sept*
while native husbands rush their mistresses
through devotions due the blue-stained hour.

Spade by shovel, earth has been moved,
old gravestones laid to rest, paving the aisle.
Dust returns to dust down a shaft of light,

devil by devil. So you'll turn back
to a life laying claim to be your own,
unbeliever shriven of all you've been while gone.

Traveler, *ou est l'Hôtel du Progrès?*
L'Hôtel du Commerce? La rue des Martyrs?
The bread, the wine, *le Burger King?*

THE HUSTLER DE PARIS

Notre Dame, Sainte Chapelle, Sacré Coeur by foot—
deep in the Louvre the Mona Lisa smirks
at the good tourist who grants her a minute
for each star in the Michelin, then soldiers on.
So all of Paris could be mine?

Quel est le prix d'entrée?
For the price of admission, I can sit in defeat
and view an *arrondissement* from home:
a small-town main street, a gas station
somewhere on a studio's back lot. A car

like a loaf of bread pulls up. Two men get out.
One's the young god, Paul Newman,
about to step into a pool hall's gloom
undubbed, only the picket fence
of French subtitles between him and us.

Like a sleepy sexton, the janitor performs
uncalled-for miracles, raising the blinds
to flood the hall with daylight
so dirty it must be divine.
"Like a church," Newman says,

"Church of the Good Hustler."
Even in black and white his eyes are blue.
The fair Savior of Western art,
devil too handsome for his own good.
The fat man with a carnation in his lapel

opens his great, soft palms
to receive the ritual talcum,
his the hands of a priest, so dainty, so mechanical.
At midnight he intones the litany of his shots.
Gray bills rain down on the gray felt.

To the gargoyles who watch, it's the old story,
boy hustles anything that moves, even pain.
La petite escourgette to mortify the flesh,
the Crown of Thorns, the Holy Sponge,
un morceau considérable of the True Cross—

that is the smell of money,
of nights just a few thousand old.
Now the saint of the broken thumbs:
"I came to play pool, Fats."
Très bien, Eddie Vite. Combien?

How much the things of this world
have darkened while we were inside.
Even the late light hurts,
the old stone cleaned of the centuries
we sat through, until it glows.

Just ahead of a last sweep by *les flics,*
street sellers roll up their rugs,
their little Winged Victories,
and weave into the nearest throng,
saints without permit passing among us.

The Later Archaic Wing

One Venus tries to loosen her marble sandal;
another disrobes as if in the next room

a bath of rock were being drawn. Without a blush,
they bare the flesh made perfect, made of stone.

Still, a Dionysus turns his sculpted back,
his the only head preserved.

Her arms missing, and her nose,
a caryatid elevates the motes and beams of dust

into the art of aging ravage by ravage.
How beautiful the old gods in their idleness,

how still. Birches hushed by snowfall
stand no closer to one another, no farther apart.

Even the light is marble in the museum
quarried from winter, carved into cloud

as cool as the goddess of love to the touch.
Even the sun god has cooled, sunning

next to a lizard hiding its fear
in the open, a stone against stone.

Into their grove a small bird has strayed.
Perched on the head of a huntress

who reaches for an arrow carved into her quiver,
it cheeps and chisels the polished air

until we are roused from the guidebook's raptures
by the bird so common we know its name,

house sparrow too tame for its own good.
A stone-faced guard has fluttered to life

beneath Winged Victory. Right wing original,
breast and left wing restored, headless,

she steams headlong into some uncarved breeze.
How like gods we are in our uselessness.

Cleopatra in the Afterworld

··

> It is my birthday,
> *I had thought t'have held it poor. But since my lord*
> *Is Antony again, I will be Cleopatra.*
> —Antony and Cleopatra

Now I rule only yesterday, she who rains
over the same river twice, sparing of her tears
the second time. Queen of darkness
laid out with jewels offered in surrender
to the invading, unconditional dark,

forty days I have been dried and do not rot.
My heart has been weighed against a feather.
Where I carried sons of men who loved
the logistics of love even more than I,
they have filled me with sand and linen bandages.

I have passed by my palace,
from the first gate of the next world
have turned around to see it a last time
as you, conquering your way east,
must have seen it from the first,

my sprawled kingdom snug up against
your outstretched palm's scarred battle-plan.
The river floods, spreading the muck
of tribute evenly though I am not there
to exact it. The asp has given me its tongue.

Fetch me my lord of hearts,
I say to my little slaves of blue clay,
that he may assemble my loosening bones
and make fast the crown grown too large.
Lady of trembling, of breaking and entering,

mourner desiring to conceal my own body,
I would be hidden bone by bone
among his imperishables.
They do not move me from the remains
of the funeral feast left in my tomb

that, under their painted-on eyes,
takes on rotten life of its own.
I am green, the lower growth of the papyrus,
the leaf laid as if fallen or carved at your feet,
carefully, so it doesn't touch your body.

I am the bird that circles over the camp
of you who keep silence in the manner
to which she is accustomed.
Though death could not spare me the tenderness
beneath contempt, I have been spared love.

A Woman on the Dump

....

> Is it peace,
> Is it a philosopher's honeymoon, one finds
> On the dump?
> —*Wallace Stevens*

Out of the cracks of cups and their handles, missing,
the leaves unceremoniously tossed, unread,
from a stubble of coffee ground ever more finely
into these hollowed grounds,

the first shift coaxes bulldozers to life,
sphinxes to tease the riddled rubble
into fresh pyramids of rot. A staleness warms enough
to waft round the lord of all purveyed.

His to count the hauls past the yawning gates
of this New Giza into the Middle Kingdom's
Late Intermediate Period. There, to purify,
to honor ourselves, we beg these offerings

of refuse be cast out. To the archaeologist
of the far-flung future, enough evidence
in the inscriptions to identify most owners:
spells scratched on the backs of envelopes

to be read out before animal sacrifice,
the milk, ground meat, beer, and soap
joined in this hereafter with the feast's remains.
Over tomatoes splitting their sides,

over a teacup stained with roses
flattened into mosaic petal from petal,
earthmovers move a little mountain
and, having moved it, move on,

overturning a diamond sprung from its ring,
glitter to a magpie's covetous eye.
If the art of loneliness is landscape,
armload by carload of black-bagged leaves,

landfill contours its likeness.

The road took us to the most distant fountain of

waters of the mighty Missouri in surch of which we

had spent so many toilsome days and wristless nights.

—Meriwether Lewis

Keats in Hampstead

....

We're too late.
The shop in the cellar is closed,
not a T-shirt, not even a ballpoint pen
or postcard to say where we've been.

But upstairs hangs a painting of his chair
next to the chair itself,
placed as in the painting, so,
next to the *faux-marbre* radiator, new,

for which we can be grateful.
An engagement ring.
Did he love the stone
for its cut, called *amandine?*

A scrap of silk left over,
perhaps, from lining the cap
of someone ordered to winter in Italy
for his health. How many shirts

did he own, who put on a clean one
when he was truly in despair?
Under a sprigged canopy,
an unmarked mound of snow—

his bed is small,
the pillows plumped, the coverlet untouched.
The mulberry tree, whose nightingale
he may have heard, has died.

The young plum in its place
shakes loose from our gaze,
all its leaves gone, its branches
floodlit, the gray of old bone.

Her nostrils are fine—
though a little painful—
her mouth bad and good—no,
the roaring of the wind

would be his wife, he'd boast.
The wind he would have drawn close
rattles the shop windows.
The high street is bitter,

the Keats Restaurant too dear,
but farther down, a tea shop
affords shelves of pastry to peruse.
Gilt-edged, embossed, the leaves

of a signature crumble against your fork.
One table over, one young American
bends to another. "And then what,"
she's dying to know, "did Shelly say to you?"

Wind Wrapped in Snow

Elder brother, younger than all of us now
  however much you age,
firstborn not answering to the name
  you can't know was yours,
first dead, old ghost, your shirt
  is too light for the season
that whitens and freezes, lightens and holds.

  Snowflake, you're out
with no coat. Listen. Stand still.
  No one is calling
across a world half-buried in snow,
  Come back, you hear me,
come back this instant, you forgot—
  the dead are selfish,

who want for nothing. We make them lie down
  in spent pastures.
To please ourselves, we lay more flowers
  and then go home
the long way, stopping for a meal.
  Brother to maggot
and the worm, you see how grief feeds itself,

  close relative to greed.
Brother to nothing, who will lie
  next to your small bones?
Wind wrapped in snow, yours is the kiss
  that stings where it lights,
melting against the cheek, it is so cold.
  You'd have none of this.

Don't let us keep you, morning star
    burning a pinprick
deep in the light years of sky.
    Nothing slows you
in your slow rise above chimney and aerial
    into another day
blank with the infant blue of oblivion.

Tapestry

On an island floating in the deepest blue,
the blue at flame's heart,

she lifts her falcon's reward,
raw meat from a gold dish,

flower heads chained into a crown,
her small sky just a flag

whose bloodied field a stream cuts,
wetting three pale crescents of moon:

a sky the red that tongues past wetness
to blister, fingers of flame

stripping canopy and understory
like old linens, the marriage

that is leaf as ruthless for light
as one who is faithful to love,

lover after lover:
the forest throbs and cracks

toward the castle and another death—
deep in the lord's kitchen

a deer carcass drips and hisses
from the spit, his men having fished it,

flaming, from the moat
whose charred banks in a fortnight

will be pierced by shoots
green with all they covet,

tender enough to eat.

Rilke in the Middle Ages

In that age the body, which was cultivated like a piece
of land, tended carefully like a harvest, and which one
owned as one owns a valuable property, was the thing
looked upon
—Rilke

He felt too much, as usual.
The woman woven into the tapestry
unwrapped a necklace, lifting it
on its cloth, no sacrament,

to show her worth as wife to the beholder.
The family lion held a tent flap open,
as did the unicorn she'd tamed
to prove she was still virginal.

Within, dark threads tangled with dark,
sweet the tortures of intimacy.
What did she have to hide?
A lady of title and some wealth,

one who could loan a castle, older—
as always in such company
he was ready to kiss the ground
she floated just above,

the suddenly close air she seemed to breathe,
kiss even her ladyship, this one nothing
if not safe for the artist intent
on spinning free of entanglements.

Cut off by a sea the shade of flame,
not the salt blue of tears well drowned,
she stood, a centuries-older woman
fading like any other, still tied

to her island knot by rotting knot.
Beyond the one hardwood, the prickly bush,
a tree of needles and a blood orange,
a red-stained sky joined seamlessly a redder sea.

Keeping a distance close enough
to pass for love, her falcon hunted a heron
through the humdrum the young Rilke was convinced
only the faithful would ever suffer,

one lady-in-waiting, one lapdog, one desire.

Les Très Riches Heures de Florida

....

NONES

At three P.M.
under sky coming to harm
something too red flashes from a limb,

so red it hurts:
against sky coming apart,
against a left-out, twice-soaked shirt,

a cardinal
inflames the profane cathedral
of suburban yard its owner let fall

into disgrace.
How rain embarrasses
the half-pruned hedge. The half-mown grass

that sports a tonsure
in reverse shines under the torture.
Rain slicks with praise red shed, red feather.

Crested seedeater
out of character where
you're neither the strictly monkish brown thrasher

nor the odd hermit thrush,
you scratch in the underbrush
of faith to see what you can flush:

a grub. A seed.
Eminence not *grise*
but *rouge*, from your lipsticked beak

you pass a sowbug
to your mate. You peck at a slug
sliming your path, seeming to beg

your forgiveness.
To what would you confess
beyond season-to-season unfaithfulness?

VESPERS

There are more divine hours:
a gold-leafed page a mower
rows with a scythe as tall as the tower

that tents aloft
a tiny sky bereft
of cloud, a chapel ceiling left

unstarred, heaven
a lake turned upside down,
filled with an emptiness that's clean

because it's cold,
glacial enough to scald
the skin it bathed, the lungs it filled.

On devotion's last page,
deep in the golden age
of illumination, the hunt's cortège

has halted at the edge
of the known world, a clearing wedged
in a forest of spears. Red bird the badge

on the huntsman's tunic,
you're the splash of crimson lake,
the distant lordship's flag, the cleric

dog's bright collar,
its heretic tongue. It slavers
on the bleeding stag. Snarling at prayer

that chases belief,
it licks the offal of grief,
the heart cast aside reward enough.

The Flowering Crab

Not the riot of flowers that is her robe,
nor the sash come loose in his hand,
not the lovers on the balcony,
turning their backs on all but each other—

no, what do they know of love beyond this?
Over their dogged ardors drift the pink
and the even pinker petals of the crab apple.
Over the curves of body tangential to body

wherever kissed, the petals brush lightly,
loss by extravagantly tiny loss
failing to cover over even the bay,
which goes on licking away the sand with salt.

Go, sweep the path of its pink,
down to the very proper dirt.
Not yet do the blue crabs come on the tide
to mate, not yet the male haul himself

onto a female to shelter her.
Three days in the claws of his embrace,
she wrestles from her shell
so that, before the new one hardens,

he may enter her. But not yet,
not yet does the crab tree's fruit stain the walk,
too sour even for the birds
driven by the cold into town to scavenge,

though it makes a fine crimson jelly.
For now, petal upon petal scums the pond,
veiling from view the ornamental carp
with nothing to chase but one another.

The Frog in the Swimming Pool

A wet green velvet scums the swimming pool,
furring the cracks. The deep end swims
in a hatful of rain, not enough to float

the bedspring barge, the tug of shopping cart.
Green-wet himself, the bullfrog holds his court,
sounding the summons to a life so low

he's yet to lure a mate. Under the lip
of concrete slab he reigns, a rumble of rock,
a flickering of sticky tongue that's licked

at any morsel winging into view.
How would he love her? Let me count the waves
that scrape the underside of night and then

let go, the depth of love unplumbed, the breadth,
the height of the pool all he needs to know.
How do I love him? Let me add the weight

of one hush to another, the mockingbird
at midnight echoing itself, not him,
one silence torn in two, sewn shut again.

Down to his level in time wings everything.
He calls the night down on his unlovely head,
on the slimy skin that breathes the slimy air—

the skin that's shed and still he is the same,
the first voice in the world, the last each night.
His call has failed to fill the empty house

across the street, the vacant swing that sways
halfheartedly, the slide slid into rust,
the old griefs waiting burial by the new.

A Field of Rape

From a field of *Brassica napus*, brassy
in full flower, best to avert the eyes.
Next to the tasteful ripening of spinach greens,

out of earth blackened where stubble burned,
winter rape shimmers in its own heat.
Waves stained acid-yellow threaten

to overrun hedgerows, but shy and turn retreat—
all but a scent so light, so full it reeks.
Down the undercurrent of stench

whirl bees industrious and wild.
Gaudiest wallflower, shimmy of *Crucifera*—
past a field of rape best to hurry.

And hurry the hired man to beat the rows
the mower readies to reap—still,
best not to think on the hare, the skylark,

the harvest mouse at nest in there.
High in the air-conditioned cab of a combine,
to the strains of a Walkman's remorseless beat,

the farmer's son will inch along the rows
he harrowed, easing the automated pillage on.
Bright flower-heads gone to seed, mown down,

lifted from windrows and mechanically flailed
until the husks, worthless, take flight
and by virtue of its greater weight

the tiny seed is saved and sold:
let rape be only what's crushed between stones
until it expels the sweet oil prized

by soap maker and machinist, by the baker
brushing his swelled-up loaves. Let only
the most expensive margarine grace their tables.

For the cattle strayed into the field,
up to their cheap neckbones in gold,
oilcake enough that they don't starve

over winter on their way to slaughter.

Like a Woman

....

> It happens that I am tired of being a man.
> —Pablo Neruda

I'm tired of being a woman. The dress-shop
   mannequin
a week's window-shopping has worn thin
has come apart at her seams,

her heavily made-up eyes still unseeing,
and just as well. Here lies her upper body,
armless, bald but for a strip of Velcro on her crown,

topped by her sleek unbending legs, her toeless feet.
Beneath her nipple-less, well-rounded breast,
someone has punched a hole where a heart should go.

Around the pile of limbs, a window dresser tiptoes,
her blistered heels revealed.
Next door's pink parlor seeps the smell of beauty,

the perfumed chemicals of the permanent
I've undergone. The matted kinks of sheep are mine,
the curls yet to relax, though I'm to rest assured.

Mirrored in the men's-store window
between two well-stuffed shirts,
arms tied behind their backs, I'm not myself.

Someone else is tired: against the palings
fencing off the boys' school,
a man in a smart gray suit is slumped,

unmanned by grief. I do what women are told to do
around a stranger. I hurry on,
sparing him the insult of my looking back.

Wracked with sobs, he looks
on some private ruin and, like a woman, weeps.

The Boy Juliet

No use my love of false noses then—
rouge to cheeks no longer in first blush,
pancake to the crows' feet coming on,

I made myself young enough to play me at fourteen,
stumbling over my dolls as I fell for a boy
from the wrong side of town.

I pitched her first, still girlish words
to the harsh-lit mirror in the dressing room:
I am here, what is your will?

My tiers of greasepaint nudged one another,
dark blue groundlings smudging gods' red lake.
The wig block never so much as blinked

from its deep breathless sleep
as that vestigial night watchman,
the stage manager, called quarter hour.

From a peephole in the faded curtain,
I glimpsed a house lit up with little dramas
played out unrehearsed by no one I recognized,

just ticket holders costumed in evening dress
who'd paid for someone else's troubles.
From those rows of inconstant moons

faceless in the dark beyond footlights' sunny glare,
mid-act I'd pick a lump of man
to court as Romeo furiously courted me.

Picking up those yards of skirt that tripped
nightly toward disaster, I'd mince my steps
to match her words. I'd pick apart a rose,

one petal Capulet, one Montague,
delivering the lines where I succumbed
to love, the contagion I was not to show

would kill before it cured. Still I think
of that boy plucking his eyebrows,
unknown first Juliet powdering the down

of his faint mustache. Padding his bony chest,
apprentice stuck in the role of yet another maiden,
the best he could get the rote promises,

when his seven years were up,
of the mouse-colored tights of a man
like the one who rushes to declaim

O *sweet Juliet, thy beauty hath made me effeminate,*
should the boy ready himself meanwhile
to die on cue once more for love.

Ovid on the Outer Cape

I paint my shaven face
the way I remember my wife made up hers
for our last night on that town,
the capital of memory, the exile's eternal city.

There are nights here, such nights,
but not much town. What there is
is narrow, a few fishermen, a few fur coats
in winter's unemployment line,

which snakes weekly through the choir loft
of the church turned public library,
the old one burned by the volunteer fireman
who always got to fires first.

Merciful the mirror that's fogged—
you wouldn't recognize this wreck
who creaks and groans, here run aground.
The foghorn bemoans its lot.

The red seaweed has been dried and crushed;
on the cheekbone is rubbed the blush of innocence,
the lips reddened to a knowing gash.
To the eyelid, lashes of mink,

glued clump by clump. My wig is frosted,
my breasts of foam uplifted.
I have poured myself into a sheath
as if, though parted,

she and I could be one body.
In her shell I teeter crabwise,
the hermit Hermaphroditus in heels,
queen of the beach,

past the O *Vacancy* sign
burning this weekend in honor
of the transvestites' convention.
The tourists gone home for the season

have nothing on us
who live at one of the ends of the earth,
at the shore of the underworld.
Who use their coins

to close the eyes of our dead
that the dead, dressed in their finest,
faces painted back to health,
have something to pay the ferryman.

The foghorn mourns longest,
not knowing what it mourns.
The stones my neighbors,
who will not have me,

lie drying into dullness
even under cloud. I send you one—
does the faintest of heartbeats ripple
under the smooth, the ageless skin?

No, the former Luftwaffe pilot
now enjoys life as a woman.
Emperor, I pray that you may always
disbelieve what I have said.

Mr. Bartram was the first to call this a garden,

but he is to be forgiven; he is an enthusiastic

botanist, and rare plants, in the eyes of such a man,

convert a wilderness at once into a garden.

—Audubon

La Petite Danseuse de Quatorze Ans

....

> *a handful of intangible ash*
> —Elizabeth Bishop

The Little Dancer, forever fourteen years,
gathers what dust she can in the museum at night,
her face upthrust as toward rain, which never appears,
cool in its caress, from the skylight's dim height.

Real gauze over flesh made bronze, she's like a saint
whose statue's dressed by nuns and set apart,
as if she could walk the flames of their votive lights
while in her hands she held her flaming heart,

not old enough to know not to make it look hard.
I thought of her as you watched some soap-opera star
sink stone by stone in a talk show's talk. It was one
A.M. You switched to Lizard Man from Mars.

He was unruffled, whipped by a wind-machine wind.
Quick! Where were more buildings for him to toss?
A bridge would have to do. Somewhere between
cold-blooded god and man the animal, he was cross.

His tail sideswiped a bus. Solemnly
he flicked a tongue that was miles too short at us.
He scaled a papery, floured, too-short peak.
Would boy meet girl? Shopping was dangerous.

My clothes lay mountainous where they fell.
Your hand was lizard-cool, I the fire
whose fever for weeks that summer burned the house.
A rocking chair to rock the flame? No, a pair

of candles that the heat had doubled up
bowed to the best dance teacher, pain. In white,
in pools of it, they sank lower still, until
they melted as I longed to from your sight.

There was no heat wave. I was all that burned.
And when I woke, it let me wake alone,
almost cold, remembering the scene
where gentle Lizard Man scaled on tiptoe down

shadow to wall to bed, then slithered out
and made me drink, and whispered, memorized,
   a handful of intangible ash
   with fixed, ignited eyes.

The Little Dancer gray in her mimicry—
no, I think sometimes of Lizard Man, the cry
of pedestrians in flight, his scaly fist
brushing a skyscraper out of the way of the sky.

The Eternal City

You search in Rome for Rome? O Traveller!
—Quevedo

THE AFTERNOON OF ROME

Room by room they close the museum
behind us, the room of clay,
the age of bronze, the small wooden box
in the shape of a sleeping deer.

It still holds a nub of charcoal
to make the eyebrows beautiful
enough to love, a few grains of rouge,
but there's to be no lingering,

not even at the feet of bride and bridegroom
reclining on their sarcophagus,
not even to remark the afterglow of dust.
The lights have been doused

in the room of candelabra—hurry!
All of Rome waits to sleep
another afternoon to ruin.
Even the laundry hangs still,

shirts carved for the statues,
no longer young, that glare
at the creaseless waiters
waiting in the wings of shadows.

Spicciati! urges the phrase book.
Your rented room waits, as quiet now
as it will ever be, the brakes, the horns
chasing church bells hour to quarter hour

papered over by the more intimate din
of *la televisione. Sbrigati!*
Forget the sights unseen;
good tourists get their money's worth

not doing what the Romans haven't done.
Look away with the exhausted tenderness
of that Etruscan groom
as you lift your hand heavily

to my heavy shoulder. Just there,
the lull that begins a lullaby,
as when the waters of traffic part
for a nun in full sail, a fleet

of tourists meek in the wake
of her dark habit. Let us lie down
and draw the map over us and sleep
a little more of our little history.

EARLY ROME

Even the women the phrase book has no phrase for
have gone to bed, from bed.
Now only a student or two are left,
rucksack or shoes for a pillow,

on the steps of the Stazione Termini.
Over an empire shrunk to a timetable,
the ticket seller yawns a universal yawn,
that much I can translate. This

is the dawn of Rome, the first train
lit up like the station's aquarium.
The neon halos of saints glow,
eels in the gloom of church porches

where electric candles burn in prayer as long
as they're paid to burn. Past the window,
the ruined baths of an emperor swim,
clouds the color of carp in a villa's pool

adrift over arches that arch for nothing,
the remains of the aqueduct.
The breakfast roll tastes of dust,
the coffee of soot, it is so good.

On the bench opposite, a madonna slumps
against a young centaur in jeans,
the old centaur eyeing her foot,
kissed smooth. In rabbit fur

the she-wolf curls
next to the delicate boy with thorn.
Keats has been laid in the dirt,
Shelley's ashes to rest in their urn.

Nothing will wake Martial the light sleeper,
or the hammerer of gold dust
he complained of. The carriage lightens,
a perfect day for decay.

Si *(scolorirà) restringerà?*
Will it (fade) shrink?
(Non) ho (niente) qualche cosa di diacharare.
I have (nothing) something to declare.

In the City of the Dead

we're tourists as dusty as old gods,
two steps behind the man from *National Geographic*
who wants a shot of the native girl he's trailed

to this pool of light fallen through the roof
of the House of the Ancient Scaffold.
She will have none of him, whose shirt
sports a fresco of bronzed bikinis and waves.

Descendants of shopkeepers, we want to see
the empire of an early villa
carved into barbarous little shops.
The last of the wine from the vineyards

that greened the slopes of Vesuvius,
much prized in the sunken garden
twice sunk, excavated from the mud.
The guard guarding the missing wall painting,

and the missing wall, has come to life,
rattling a ring of rusty keys
until a door groans on its ancient hinge—
the Small-Appliance Repair Shop,

where a broken candelabrum has had centuries
to tarnish next to a small fallen god.
In the city of the dead, the living dig,
the dead do as they are bid.

They stay in the next room,
they stay still, ladies veiled
from the eyes of strangers, nothing to be seen
of the seamstress but her thimble.

A blackened pear left behind by a juggler.
A crumpled statuette, the goddess of love
taking forever to undo her sandal.
Here let love burn scratched in a wall.

No one, not even a fortune teller,
has remarked our arrival, we are so godlike now.
In the city of the dead, we're offered passage,
not yet dug, to another buried street.

The Dictionary of Silence

And in that city the houses of the dead
are left empty, if the dead are famous enough;
by day the living pay to see if dust is all
  that befalls the lives they left behind.

Coating even the glassed-in waistcoat in time,
coloring the air of the room stripped bare,
down four stories of twisted stair it falls,
  down on the dictionary no longer there.

Empty your pockets,
empty your hearts, that empty upper room exhorts.
Forget the scrap of paper with the missing word
  for what's missing—

go home to your rented room.
Go on. Six cramped quills, one elbow chair, missing
    a leg,
held up all those years by Johnson's willing it to hold
  his bulk—now even the "soul hath *elbowroom*"

in that room where scribes scribbled out that quote.
In that city the dead never want to get up,
just as in life. What can we offer them?
  Just this dust to cover them deeper,

kin to the soot that shadowed their days.
Kiss from a wife who no longer wanted to be touched—
love, he held, regarded with passionate affection,
  like one sex to the other, first; or, second,

made do with the affection of a friend; or
managed merely parental tenderness, third; or, fourth,
no more than pleasure with, delighting in; or, fifth,
    no less than the reverent unwillingness to offend.

O had a long sound, as in *alone*. Her *opium*.
On clean-shirt day he would pay a visit to his wife.
Pack meant *large bundle of any thing*—"on your head
    a *pack* of sorrows."

Quiet. The square just off Fleet Street
so *quiet* Carlyle got lost on his way there.
Remember the garret floorboards' complaint, the
        muffled
    ruffling of pigeons just overhead?

Such silence we fell into
stair by stair, the house to ourselves.
Tired of London, he claimed, and one was
    tired of life. Were we just tired?

Under the low ceiling as below deck,
up where no angle was true, we sank in deeper silence,
valedictory, the way it took us in.
    Volumes of ancient air closed around us, blank,

weighted by the latest dust.
What had we come to the house of the dead to see?
    Something
exotic? The zebra presented to the queen in 1726?
    Something
    exactly as it might have been? Did you

yawn first, back among the living?
You pulled me from traffic rushing downstream
    instead of up,
that Zambezi best forded from stripe to painted stripe,
    a "zebra crossing." I'd looked the wrong way.

Persephone in the West

Down some long, unseen staircase of air
  the plane bumped,
and we were through with cloud. On the sky floor
  was laid the desert of childhood,
a Christmas train set gathering dust.
  The last of the snow

clung to the north of every little rise
  toy cars drove around
past clumps of sagebrush, past tumbleweeds
  stuck to chain-link fence,
another record crop. How long till the chinook?
  I don't want to be wakened,

lost in my old single bed, by the warm wind
  I always forget I know by heart.
Winter sunrise sketching a briefly rosy day—
  I don't want it to reveal
the return of the lawn, scraggly, pale,
  sporting the first bloom,

a long-lost mitten whose mate's gone missing.
  Snowmen brought to their knees—
how quickly the spring I always seem to bring
  from the underworld bores.
Boys I went to school with, shedding their hats and coats—
  they've fattened, or lost hair, or both.

From ancient stables to upstart shopping mall
  their daughters flock.
To her well-stocked feeder, Mother attracts the birds
  on their way farther north,

calling me by my sister's name to see
    the rare such-and-such,

another little bird in brilliant camouflage,
    the shades of dirt.
Canada geese have claimed the first tender shoots,
    tuft by devoured tuft.
The dogwoods of the underworld are shivering
        by now,
    petals snowier than snow,

the jaded hands of palm fronds clapping.
    The crimson tedium, acid-sweet,
that marries seed from seed—I want the upper world
    to freeze, outlined in frost
at once delicate and witheringly accurate,
    want wild pomegranates

the sweetly unreasoning red of stoplights
    to flare their ripeness
beside the road. I want to taste again
    that moment in the underworld
I touched its fruit. I want us to stop,
    my mother and me,

though I'll have a flight to catch,
    the plane to shadow
the River Styx where it trails
    through northern Florida,
fair the tailwind in the ferryman's favor,
    lost time to be made good.

The Sadness of the Subtropics

....

I went as far as the earth allows one to go.
—Lévi-Strauss, Tristes Tropiques

A last breath has been dug
from the pale sand and held,
the open grave as deep
as the earth allows one to go.

Shallow in the shallows of sand,
it holds its sides against the slide
of tears grain by grain
over the outspread welcome of roots,

cut back to make a little room.
The white truck is sad,
the white folding-chairs
tilting their headstones in the white sand,

the plastic flowers that whiten,
theirs life everlasting, rotten life.
Even the palmettos are sad
for they have nothing to mourn,

the earth theirs to inherit.
The black vestments of flies
cross and recross the stench of sadness
and will not let it go.

Where two or three are gathered—
between this world and the next,
vultures hover on wings of crepe,
attentive to our every need.

Someone has raked the leaves and then the sand,
the bed of ashes still warm,
a last leaf raised up on a breath
of wind, twirled, and let fall.

The distant traffic is sad, a rush
of waves over a fossil sea,
down the highway just through the trees.
You who are weary, come home.

Air-Conditioned Air

Of windows closing on muslin curtains
so they no longer swelled into hoop skirts
or swooned across love seats

the night a taxi raced from lab to lodgings,
men in white coats thrusting a bundled blanket
at a dreamer—their swaddled ice

the first from his machine. Farewell,
ceiling fans that propelled interim regimes
into torrid zones, palm courts

fawning over wilted colonials,
aspics weeping onto the native greens.
Farewell, the flies that tended leftover meat.

Like servants shooed from table,
they wove shadow to shadow
through the vestigial dusk.

It is late. The street light
lies fair upon the strait, on the coast
of Florida it gleams. Sea turtles lay their eggs

in the parking lots of hotels
glimmering and vast—come to the window,
air-conditioned is the night air,

you can hear the comfort of its roar
begin to chill and then begin again,
the flow of something human drowning the sea

somewhere far below our room.
The air is calm tonight, the same air as tomorrow,
and we are here. Look how the little candelabra

of a pleasure boat is borne by the darkness
of water through the earthly dark
over the old slave route.

Briar Rose

....

Where is paradise without the gate?
Ask any gardener, his bags of bone meal busy
    keeping the weedy world at bay.

Within its boxwood walls, like that great kitchen
    the cook hungered after,
a place for everything, and everything in it

    named by scholar and scullery maid:
between *Rosa canina* and *foetida*, next to "Adam"
    and "Little White Pet," the briar

a mother's thorned thanksgiving named me for,
    pricking the very air's approach.
Ask any man with sense enough not to try for me

    that century I slept in state:
men who did wound up as bones of stories
    tendril by barbed tendril woven,

sentence by overgrown sentence, into mine—
    all but you, the thicket parting,
thorns going soft as you breezed past.

    What is paradise without a gate?
I slept the sleep of that first man who slept so deep
    he didn't miss the bone he gave up.

What must his waking words have been? *Is it you?*
    How long you have kept me waiting.
I give him mine. Given back a voice gone feral,

that squeaked and croaked,
I gave you a talking-to cut off by your long—
    no, the briefest kiss.

Think of your gardens when we're not there.
    No longer does the moorhen cross the pond
on stepping stones of lily pads that if it rushes

    bear its feathered weight.

Under Cancer

I

How he loves his patch of lawn,
grooming it with scissors
blade by stray blade.
There is no joy as indifferent as his,

this half-Noah who has one of everything:
one rose, one thorn, one small bed
of onions under their new name,
ripening to make you weep.

His accent still as heavy as black bread,
he has made landfall here,
where the one poppy blushes with rage
to pronounce each petal perfectly.

It's still raining in the past,
falling in clean sheets over the rust
of old rain, slumping the mattress
flung out, scented with must.

A lone blackbird braves the polished grass,
cocking his head, straining to hear the worm
that tunnels from dark to darker,
the gardener in its debt

for the earth moved, each mouthful of dirt.
Rain after long rainfall, so light,
all that was loved being wet or dead.

2

By first light you lost yourself at last
to sleep, held under, soothed
until you were smoothed into a boy again.

Back in your father's house,
your father back from the dead,
comparing dust with dust and earth with earth

like any sparrow that has cleansed itself,
a flutter of feathers in a wallow of dirt,
like any man who, bathed, has been laid underground.

The Crab was in its heaven. At its heart
swam stars so faint of magnitude
even the driest eye could not resolve them

into more than a furious, blurred swarm.
The first star of evening still burned hottest,
turning the Lyre white-blue

in the empty hands of Orpheus—
you bring nothing into this world,
nothing you can carry from the next.

In the wake of the dustmen hauling ashes to ash
through the ashen dawn,
the soul is trundled by wagon

to where it's let go.

The Garden

The ducks have turned to stone, the lovers untwined
 and straggled to their separate beds.
Blossom upon lush blossom closes in on itself,

 the gardener closing the Carnivorous House,
the Venus flytrap close-lipped over a last luckless fly.
 Night-blooming cereus opens

to a world ever more shadowed, more dimly seen.
 Go back calls a thrush from the bramble hedge.
Think of that first garden after the gates were closed,

 paradise retaken by weeds once damned.
Around the poisonous buttercup, cows have chewed
 and now lie, stately, in a patch of shade.

In place of tears, the corners of their unblinking eyes
 are crawling with flies.
And there is evening and there is morning, an
 eighth day.

Invitation to the Past

Closer, a little closer. There.
The clouded mirror, peeling.
A blue three-legged bureau.
The narrow bed made up afresh by snow.

How much to clear away that room
lit by snow's soft cold light?
Someone was happy there,
as happy as sad, or not so sad,

but who? The one I remember
as if it were someone else,
who dried her eyes and cried.
Just clear the kitchen table,

snowed under, the newspaper's white pillow,
the ugly rug where we lay
unmoving in the unmoved air
of a muggy night, spent by love.

A floor below, the oboist rehearsed
the only phrase he seemed to know.
No two alike, flake after frozen flake
skirls down upon his ghost orchestra.

Lightly, crystal on barbed crystal,
the snow of forgetting falls
on already forgotten snow,
a tenderness so selfish

its watery tonnage weighs
against what love I would claim
I felt, finding it wanting,
snow over dust, ash under snow.

Illinois Poetry Series   *Laurence Lieberman, Editor*

....

Cities in Motion
  Sylvia Moss (1987)
Selected by Derek Walcott

The Hand of God and a Few
Bright Flowers
  William Olsen (1988)
Selected by David Wagoner

The Great Bird of Love
  Paul Zimmer (1989)
Selected by William Stafford

Stubborn
  Roland Flint (1990)
Selected by Dave Smith

The Surface
  Laura Mullen (1991)
Selected by C. K. Williams

The Dig
  Lynn Emanuel (1992)
Selected by Gerald Stern

My Alexandria
  Mark Doty (1993)
Selected by Philip Levine

The High Road to Taos
  Martin Edmunds (1994)
Selected by Donald Hall

OTHER POETRY VOLUMES

Her Soul beneath the Bone:
Women's Poetry on Breast Cancer
  Edited by Leatrice Lifshitz (1988)

Days from a Dream Almanac
  Dennis Tedlock (1990)

Working Classics: Poems on
Industrial Life
  Edited by Peter Oresick
  and Nicholas Coles (1990)

Hummers, Knucklers, and
Slow Curves: Contemporary
Baseball Poems
  Edited by Don Johnson (1991)

The Double Reckoning of
Christopher Columbus
  Barbara Helfgott Hyett (1992)

Selected Poems
  Jean Garrigue (1992)

New and Selected Poems, 1962–92
  Laurence Lieberman (1993)